To: Mrs. Phillips

From: Nicole Martinez

Teachers Have Class

A tribute

EDITED BY MARY RODARTE

Andrews McMeel Publishing, LLC
Kansas City • Sydney • London

This 2011 edition printed for Barnes & Noble, Inc.,
by Andrews McMeel Publishing, LLC

Andrews McMeel Publishing, LLC
an Andrews McMeel Universal company
1130 Walnut Street, Kansas City, Missouri 64106

www.andrewsmcmeel.com

ISBN: 978-1-4494-0827-5

ATTENTION: SCHOOLS AND BUSINESSES

Andrews McMeel books are available at quantity discounts with bulk purchase for educational, business, or sales promotional use. For information, please e-mail the Andrews McMeel Publishing Special Sales Department:
specialsales@amuniversal.com

❦ CONTENTS ❧

INTRODUCTION

Everyone who remembers his own educational experience remembers teachers, not methods and techniques.

— SIDNEY HOOK

WE ALL HAVE HEROES in our lives—those whom we admire and perhaps strive to emulate. They inspire us to reach for greatness, to achieve our goals, and to make them (and ourselves) proud.

In a world where change is the norm, our teachers are sources of constancy: mentors who guide us, spark our curiosity, open doors for us, and let us see our future. When our determination flags, teachers are there to encourage, prompting us, "You can do it!"

Even when we're grown and teachers are no longer part of our daily lives, their wise lessons—do your homework, don't give up, and never, never cheat!—remain with us.

We've all had teachers we'll never forget: the one who stayed after school to help us with a difficult subject, the one who imbued us with self-confidence, the one who told us we *could* when we were certain we couldn't. These are the teachers we call *heroes,* and this collection is a heartfelt tribute to them.

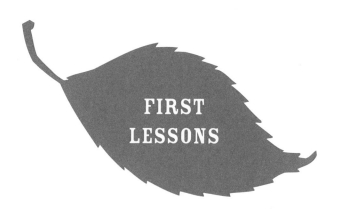

FIRST
LESSONS

The art of teaching is the art of assisting discovery.

—MARK VAN DOREN

IF YOU PRACTICE AN ART, BE PROUD OF IT AND MAKE IT PROUD OF YOU. . . . IT MAY BREAK YOUR HEART, BUT IT WILL FILL YOUR HEART BEFORE IT BREAKS IT: IT WILL MAKE YOU A PERSON IN YOUR OWN RIGHT.

—MAXWELL ANDERSON

To have ideas is to gather flowers. To think is to weave them into garlands.

—ANNE-SOPHIE SWETCHINE

I CONSIDER A HUMAN SOUL WITHOUT EDU-
CATION LIKE MARBLE IN A QUARRY, WHICH
SHOWS NONE OF ITS INHERENT BEAUTIES
UNTIL THE SKILL OF THE POLISHER SKETCHES
OUT THE COLORS, MAKES THE SURFACE SHINE,
AND DISCOVERS EVERY ORNAMENTAL CLOUD,
SPOT, AND VEIN THAT RUNS THROUGH IT.

—JOSEPH ADDISON

IT IS THE TRAINED, LIVING HUMAN SOUL, CULTIVATED AND STRENGTHENED BY LONG STUDY AND THOUGHT, THAT BREATHES THE REAL BREATH OF LIFE INTO BOYS AND GIRLS AND MAKES THEM HUMAN, WHETHER THEY BE BLACK OR WHITE, GREEK, RUSSIAN, OR AMERICAN.

—W. E. B. DuBois

It is the supreme art of

the teacher to awaken joy

in creative expression

and knowledge.

—ALBERT EINSTEIN

Not just part of us becomes a teacher. It engages the whole self—the woman or man, wife or husband, mother or father, the lover, scholar or artist in you as well as the teacher earning money.

—Sylvia Ashton-Warner

THE MEDIOCRE TEACHER TELLS. THE GOOD TEACHER EXPLAINS. THE SUPERIOR TEACHER DEMONSTRATES. THE GREAT TEACHER INSPIRES.

—WILLIAM ARTHUR WARD

LIFE IS AMAZING, AND THE TEACHER HAD BETTER PREPARE HIMSELF TO BE A MEDIUM FOR THAT AMAZEMENT.

—EDWARD BLISHEN

The brighter you are,
the more you have to learn.

—DON HEROLD

I HAVE NO RICHES BUT MY THOUGHTS,

YET THESE ARE WEALTH ENOUGH FOR ME.

—SARA TEASDALE

Ah, but a man's reach should exceed his grasp

Or what's a heaven for?

—Robert Browning

*By learning you
will teach; by teaching
you will learn.*

—LATIN PROVERB

Teach the tongue to say

"I do not know."

—MAIMONIDES

THE SECRET OF JOY IN WORK IS CONTAINED IN ONE WORD—EXCELLENCE. TO KNOW HOW TO DO SOMETHING WELL IS TO ENJOY IT.

—PEARL BUCK

ACCEPTANCE OF PREVAILING STANDARDS OFTEN MEANS WE HAVE NO STANDARDS OF OUR OWN.

—JEAN TOOMER

NEVER SEEM MORE LEARNED THAN THE PEOPLE YOU ARE WITH. WEAR YOUR LEARNING LIKE A POCKET WATCH AND KEEP IT HIDDEN. DO NOT PUT IT OUT TO COUNT THE HOURS, BUT GIVE THE TIME WHEN YOU ARE ASKED.

—EARL OF CHESTERFIELD

Men too involved in details

usually become unable to deal

with great matters.

—François de la Rochefoucauld

WHAT GREATER OR BETTER GIFT CAN WE OFFER THE REPUBLIC THAN TO TEACH AND INSTRUCT OUR YOUNG?

—CICERO

THE TRUTH OF IT IS, THE FIRST RUDI-
MENTS OF EDUCATION ARE GIVEN VERY
INDISCREETLY BY MOST PARENTS.

—SIR RICHARD STEELE

PRESUMPTION SHOULD NEVER MAKE US NEGLECT THAT WHICH APPEARS EASY TO US, NOR DESPAIR MAKE US LOSE COURAGE AT THE SIGHT OF DIFFICULTIES.

—BENJAMIN BANNEKER

THE GIFT OF TEACHING IS A PECULIAR TALENT, AND IMPLIES A NEED AND A CRAVING IN THE TEACHER HIMSELF.

—JOHN JAY CHAPMAN

THE WILL TO SUCCEED IS IMPORTANT, BUT WHAT'S EVEN MORE IMPORTANT IS THE WILL TO PREPARE.

—BOBBY KNIGHT

No one rises to

low expectations.

—JESSE JACKSON

Everybody is now so

busy teaching that nobody

has any time to learn.

—AGNES REPPLIER

THE JOB OF A TEACHER IS TO EXCITE IN THE YOUNG A BOUNDLESS SENSE OF CURIOSITY ABOUT LIFE, SO THAT THE GROWING CHILD SHALL COME TO APPREHEND IT WITH AN EXCITEMENT TEMPERED BY AWE AND WONDER.

—JOHN GARRETT

Men learn while they teach.

—SENECA

A professor must have a

theory as a dog must

have fleas.

—H. L. MENCKEN

MEN MUST BE TAUGHT AS IF YOU TAUGHT THEM NOT,

AND THINGS UNKNOWN PROPOSED AS THINGS FORGOT.

—ALEXANDER POPE

THE MERE IMPARTING OF INFORMATION IS NOT EDUCATION. ABOVE ALL THINGS, THE EFFORT MUST RESULT IN MAKING A MAN THINK AND DO FOR HIMSELF.

—CARTER G. WOODSON

A SUCCESSFUL TEACHER NEEDS: THE EDU-CATION OF A COLLEGE PRESIDENT, THE EXECUTIVE ABILITY OF A FINANCIER, THE HU-MILITY OF A DEACON, THE ADAPTABILITY OF A CHAMELEON, THE HOPE OF AN OPTIMIST, THE COURAGE OF A HERO, THE WISDOM OF A SERPENT, THE GENTLENESS OF A DOVE, THE PATIENCE OF JOB, THE GRACE OF GOD, AND THE PERSISTENCE OF THE DEVIL.

—ANONYMOUS

Training is everything. The peach was once a bitter almond; cauliflower is nothing but cabbage with a college education.

—Mark Twain

*The difference between
you and me is that you think
to live and I live to think.*

—DOROTHY M. RICHARDSON

I hold it true that thoughts are things
Endowed with bodies, breath, and wings.

—ELLA WHEELER WILCOX

The difficult we do

immediately; the impossible

takes a little longer.

—U.S. ARMY SLOGAN

The vanity of teaching
often tempteth a man to forget
he is a blockhead.

—GEORGE SAVILE

We teach what we

need to learn.

—GLORIA STEINEM

THE TEACHER'S LIFE SHOULD HAVE THREE PERIODS—STUDY UNTIL TWENTY-FIVE, INVESTIGATION UNTIL FORTY, PROFESSION UNTIL SIXTY, AT WHICH AGE I WOULD HAVE HIM RETIRED ON A DOUBLE ALLOWANCE.

—SIR WILLIAM OSLER

Teaching consists of equal parts perspiration, inspiration, and resignation.

—SUSAN OHANIAN

B E WILLING TO MAKE DECISIONS. THAT'S THE MOST IMPORTANT QUALITY IN A GOOD LEADER. DON'T FALL VICTIM TO WHAT I CALL THE "READY-AIM-AIM-AIM-AIM SYNDROME." YOU MUST BE WILLING TO FIRE.

—T. BOONE PICKENS

The way to get things done
is not to mind who gets the
credit of doing them.

—BENJAMIN JOWETT

*Teachers are more
than any other class the
guardians of civilization.*

—BERTRAND RUSSELL

FOR EVERY PERSON WHO WANTS TO TEACH THERE ARE APPROXIMATELY THIRTY WHO DON'T WANT TO LEARN—MUCH.

—W. C. SELLAR AND R. J. YEATMAN

Teaching is the royal road to learning.

—JESSAMYN WEST

The object of teaching a child

is to enable him to get

along without a teacher.

—Elbert Hubbard

TO NOURISH CHILDREN AND RAISE THEM AGAINST ODDS IS IN ANY TIME, ANY PLACE, MORE VALUABLE THAN TO FIX BOLTS IN CARS OR DESIGN NUCLEAR WEAPONS.

—MARILYN FRENCH

TEACHING IS AN INSTINCTUAL ART, MINDFUL OF POTENTIAL, CRAVING OF REALIZATIONS, A PAUSING, SEAMLESS PROCESS.

—A. BARTLETT GIAMATTI

FOLLOW THE PATH OF THE UNSAFE, INDE-PENDENT THINKER. EXPOSE YOUR IDEAS TO THE DANGERS OF CONTROVERSY. SPEAK YOUR MIND AND FEAR LESS THE LABEL OF "CRACKPOT" THAN THE STIGMA OF CONFORM-ITY. AND ON ISSUES THAT SEEM IMPORTANT TO YOU, STAND UP AND BE COUNTED AT ANY COST.

—THOMAS J. WATSON

Good teaching is one-fourth preparation and three-fourths theater.

—GAIL GODWIN

A TEACHER'S DAY IS HALF BUREAUCRACY, HALF CRISIS, HALF MONOTONY, AND ONE-EIGHTIETH EPIPHANY. NEVER MIND THE ARITHMETIC.

—SUSAN OHANIAN

What we have to learn

to do, we learn by doing.

—ARISTOTLE

GOOD TEACHERS ARE GLAD WHEN A TERM BEGINS AND A LITTLE SAD WHEN IT ENDS. THEY REMEMBER SOME OF THEIR STUDENTS FOR MANY YEARS, AND THEIR STUDENTS REMEMBER THEM. THEY NEVER MAKE ASSUMPTIONS ABOUT WHAT THEIR PUPILS KNOW; THEY TAKE THE TROUBLE TO FIND OUT, AND THEY ARE TIRELESS IN FINDING NEW WAYS OF REPEATING WHERE REPETITION IS NECESSARY.

—MARGARET MEAD

A professor is one who talks

in someone else's sleep.

—W. H. Auden

THE WHOLE ART OF TEACHING IS ONLY THE ART OF AWAKENING THE NATURAL CURIOSITY OF YOUNG MINDS FOR THE PURPOSE OF SATISFYING IT AFTERWARDS.

—ANATOLE FRANCE

MAN IS THE ONLY ONE THAT KNOWS NOTHING, THAT CAN LEARN NOTHING WITHOUT BEING TAUGHT. HE CAN NEITHER SPEAK NOR TALK NOR EAT, AND IN SHORT HE CAN DO NOTHING AT THE PROMPTING OF NATURE ONLY, BUT WEEP.

—PLINY THE ELDER

To teach is to touch

lives forever.

—ANONYMOUS

If we succeed in giving the love of learning, the learning itself is sure to follow.

—JOHN LUBBOCK

A GOOD TEACHER IS ONE WHO HELPS YOU BECOME WHO YOU FEEL YOURSELF TO BE. A GOOD TEACHER IS ALSO ONE WHO SAYS SOMETHING YOU WON'T UNDERSTAND UNTIL TEN YEARS LATER.

—JULIUS LESTER

THE WORLD OF LEARNING IS SO BROAD, AND THE HUMAN SOUL IS SO LIMITED IN POWER! WE REACH FORTH AND STRAIN EVERY NERVE, BUT WE SEIZE ONLY A BIT OF THE CURTAIN THAT HIDES THE INFINITE FROM US.

—MARIA MITCHELL

Teacher:

The child's third parent.

—Hyman Maxwell Berston

Bᵁᵀ ᵀᴼ ᴳᴼ ᵀᴼ school ᴵᴺ ᴬ summer morn,

Oh, it drives all joy away!

Under a cruel eye outworn,

The little ones spend the day—

In sighing and dismay.

—William Blake

One good teacher in a lifetime
may sometimes change a
delinquent into a solid citizen.

—PHILIP WYLIE

ALWAYS BEHAVE LIKE A DUCK—KEEP
CALM AND UNRUFFLED ON THE SURFACE
BUT PADDLE LIKE THE DEVIL UNDERNEATH.

—LORD BARBIZON

He that teaches us anything which we knew not before is undoubtedly to be reverenced as a master.

—Samuel Johnson

THE TEACHER'S TASK IS NOT TO IMPLANT FACTS BUT TO PLACE THE SUBJECT TO BE LEARNED IN FRONT OF THE LEARNER AND, THROUGH SYMPATHY, EMOTION, IMAGINATION, AND PATIENCE, TO AWAKEN IN THE LEARNER THE RESTLESS DRIVE FOR ANSWERS AND INSIGHTS WHICH ENLARGE THE PERSONAL LIFE AND GIVE IT MEANING.

—NATHAN M. PUSEY

FOUR YEARS WAS ENOUGH OF HARVARD. I STILL HAD A LOT TO LEARN, BUT HAD BEEN GIVEN THE LIBERATING NOTION THAT NOW I COULD TEACH MYSELF.

—JOHN UPDIKE

*We have need of very
little learning to have
a good mind.*

—Michel Eyquem de Montaigne

What was the duty of the

teacher if not to inspire?

—BHARATI MUKHERJEE

HUMAN BEINGS ARE FULL OF EMOTION, AND THE TEACHER WHO KNOWS HOW TO USE IT WILL HAVE DEDICATED LEARNERS. IT MEANS SENDING DOMINANT SIGNALS INSTEAD OF SUBMISSIVE ONES WITH YOUR EYES, BODY, AND VOICE.

—LEON LESSINGER

The task of a teacher is not
to work for the pupil nor
to oblige him to work, but to
show him how to work.

—WANDA LANDOWSKA

A good teacher, like a good entertainer first must hold his audience's attention. Then he can teach his lesson.

—JOHN HENDRIK CLARKE

Blessed is he who has found his work; let him ask no other blessedness.

—THOMAS CARLYLE

I F YOU WOULD BE A REAL SEEKER AFTER TRUTH, IT IS NECESSARY THAT AT LEAST ONCE IN YOUR LIFE YOU DOUBT, AS FAR AS POSSIBLE, ALL THINGS.

—RENÉ DESCARTES

As with all great teachers, his curriculum was an insignificant part of what he communicated. From him you didn't learn a subject, but life. . . . Tolerance and justice, fearlessness and pride, reverence and pity, are learned in a course on long division if the teacher has those qualities . . .

—WILLIAM ALEXANDER PERCY

I MIGHT HAVE DISSECTED A FROG FIVE HUNDRED TIMES, BUT THE 501ST TIME I ALWAYS SEE SOMETHING I DIDN'T BEFORE— AND IT'S THE SAME THING WITH TEACHING STUDENTS. YOU ALWAYS SEE SOMETHING NEW.

—ANNE FRYE

Teaching is not a lost art,
but regard for it is a
lost tradition.

—JACQUES BARZUN

In teaching it is the method

and not the content that is

the message . . . the drawing

out, not the pumping in.

—ASHLEY MONTAGUE

WE SHOULD BE CAREFUL TO GET OUT OF AN EXPERIENCE ONLY THE WISDOM THAT IS IN IT—AND STOP THERE; LEST WE BE LIKE THE CAT THAT SITS DOWN ON A HOT STOVE-LID. SHE WILL NEVER SIT DOWN ON A HOT STOVE-LID AGAIN—AND THAT IS WELL; BUT ALSO SHE WILL NEVER SIT DOWN ON A COLD ONE ANYMORE.

—MARK TWAIN

To teach is to

learn twice.

—JOSEPH JOUBERT

Our life is frittered away by detail. . . . Simplify, simplify.

—HENRY DAVID THOREAU

But it is not hard work which is dreary; it is superficial work. That is always boring in the long run, and it has always seemed strange to me that in our endless discussions about education so little stress is ever laid on the pleasure of becoming an educated person, the enormous interest it adds to life. To be able to be caught up into the world of thought—that is to be educated.

—Edith Hamilton

*To talk in public, to think
in solitude, to read and to hear,
to inquire and answer inquiries,
is the business of the scholar.*

—SAMUEL JOHNSON

What constitutes

the teachers is the passion

to make scholars.

—GEORGE HERBERT PALMER

As we read the school reports on our children, we realize a sense of relief that can rise to delight that—thank heaven—nobody is reporting in this fashion on us.

—J. B. Priestley

FIFTY YEARS AGO TEACHERS SAID THEIR TOP DISCIPLINE PROBLEMS WERE TALKING, CHEWING GUM, MAKING NOISE, AND RUNNING IN THE HALLS. THE CURRENT LIST, BY CONTRAST, SOUNDS LIKE A CROSS BETWEEN A RAP SHEET AND THE SEVEN DEADLY SINS.

—ANNA QUINDLEN

THAT ALONE IS LIBERAL KNOWLEDGE, WHICH STANDS ON ITS OWN PRETEN-SIONS, WHICH IS INDEPENDENT OF SEQUEL, EXPECTS NO COMPLEMENT, REFUSES TO BE *INFORMED* . . . BY ANY END, OR ABSORBED INTO ANY ART, IN ORDER DULY TO PRESENT ITSELF TO OUR CONTEMPLATION.

—JOHN HENRY NEWMAN

It is a greater work to

educate a child, in the true

and larger sense of the word,

than to rule a state.

—William Ellery Channing

THE ART
OF TEACHING

I touch the future.

I teach.

—CHRISTA MCAULIFFE

I'M NEVER GOING TO BE A MOVIE STAR. BUT THEN, IN ALL PROBABILITY, LIZ TAYLOR IS NEVER GOING TO TEACH FIRST AND SECOND GRADE.

—MARY J. WILSON,
ELEMENTARY SCHOOL TEACHER

My heart is singing for joy this morning. A miracle has happened! The light of understanding has shone upon my little pupil's mind, and behold, all things are changed!

—ANNIE SULLIVAN

D ELIGHTFUL TASK! TO REAR THE TENDER THOUGHT,

TO TEACH THE YOUNG IDEA HOW TO SHOOT.

—JAMES THOMSON

I do not teach children,
I give them joy.

—ISADORA DUNCAN

A TEACHER WHO IS ATTEMPTING TO TEACH WITHOUT INSPIRING THE PUPIL WITH A DESIRE TO LEARN IS HAMMERING ON COLD IRON.

—HORACE MANN

Never give up and

never give in.

—HUBERT H. HUMPHREY

Good is not good,

where better is expected.

—THOMAS FULLER

The truth is that I am
enslaved . . . in one vast love
affair with seventy children.

—SYLVIA ASHTON-WARNER

I am teaching. . . . It's kind

of like having a love affair

with a rhinoceros.

—ANNE SEXTON

THEORIES AND GOALS OF EDUCATION DON'T MATTER A WHIT IF YOU DON'T CONSIDER YOUR STUDENTS TO BE HUMAN BEINGS.

—LOU ANN WALKER

The first and great

commandment is,

Don't let them scare you.

—ELMER DAVIS

When a teacher calls a boy

by his entire name it means

trouble.

—MARK TWAIN

IN EXAMINATIONS THOSE WHO DO NOT WISH TO KNOW ASK QUESTIONS OF THOSE WHO CANNOT TELL.

—SIR WALTER RALEIGH

WHEN YOU DO KNOW SOMETHING ABOUT THE REALITY OF THE WORLD THAT THOSE WHO STAND IN IGNORANCE DO NOT KNOW, THEN YOU CAN'T NOT EDUCATE.

—BETTY POWELL

WE MUST NOT, IN TRYING TO THINK ABOUT HOW WE CAN MAKE A BIG DIFFERENCE, IGNORE THE SMALL DAILY DIFFERENCES WE CAN MAKE WHICH, OVER TIME, ADD UP TO BIG DIFFERENCES THAT WE OFTEN CANNOT FORESEE.

—MARIAN WRIGHT EDELMAN

Don't limit a child to your own learning, for he was born in another time.

—RABBINICAL SAYING

R ING THE BELLS THAT STILL CAN RING.

FORGET YOUR PERFECT OFFERING.

THERE IS A CRACK IN EVERYTHING.

THAT'S HOW THE LIGHT GETS IN.

—LEONARD COHEN

I see the mind of the five-year-old as a volcano with two vents: destructiveness and creativeness.

—SYLVIA ASHTON-WARNER

MIX WITH YOUR SAGE COUNSELS SOME BRIEF FOLLY.

IN DUE PLACE TO FORGET ONE'S WISDOM IS SWEET.

—CICERO

IT IS HARD TO CONVINCE A HIGH-SCHOOL STUDENT THAT HE WILL ENCOUNTER A LOT OF PROBLEMS MORE DIFFICULT THAN THOSE OF ALGEBRA AND GEOMETRY.

—EDGAR W. HOWE

In real life, I assure you, there is no such thing as algebra.

—FRAN LEBOWITZ

*Children should be led into
the right paths, not by severity,
but by persuasion.*

—TERENCE

TO KNOW HOW TO SUGGEST IS THE GREAT ART OF TEACHING. TO ATTAIN IT WE MUST BE ABLE TO GUESS WHAT WILL INTEREST; WE MUST LEARN TO READ THE CHILDISH SOUL AS WE MIGHT A PIECE OF MUSIC.

—H. F. AMIEL

The shell must be cracked

apart if what is in it is to

come out, for if you want

the kernel you must break

the shell.

—MEISTER ECKHART

As plants are suffocated and drowned with too much moisture, and lamps with too much oil, so is the active part of the understanding with too much study.

—Michel Eyquem de Montaigne

This will never be a civilized country until we expend more money for books than we do for chewing gum.

—ELBERT HUBBARD

We cannot always build

the future for our youth,

but we can build our youth

for the future.

—FRANKLIN D. ROOSEVELT

Learning is not child's play; we cannot learn without pain.

—ARISTOTLE

Too often we give children answers to remember rather than problems to solve.

—ROGER LEWIN

Teach the young
people how to think,
not what to think.

—SIDNEY SUGARMAN

Spoon feeding in the long run teaches us nothing but the shape of the spoon.

—E. M. FORSTER

*Not failure, but
low aim, is crime.*

—JAMES RUSSELL LOWELL

It is good to have an end

to journey toward; but it's

the journey that matters,

in the end.

—Ursula K. Le Guin

Great thoughts come

from the heart.

—MARQUIS DE VAUVENARGUES

All want to be learned,
but no one is willing to pay
the price.

—JUVENAL

What we want is to see the child in pursuit of knowledge, and not knowledge in pursuit of the child.

—George Bernard Shaw

Don't try to fix the students, fix ourselves first. The good teacher makes the poor student good and the good student superior. When our students fail, we, as teachers, too, have failed.

—Marva Collins

Don't set your wit

against a child.

—JONATHAN SWIFT

We teachers can only help

the work going on, as servants

wait upon a master.

—MARIA MONTESSORI

Children are unpredictable.
You never know what
inconsistency they're going to
catch you in next.

—FRANKLIN P. JONES

*Don't let your will
roar when your power
only whispers.*

—THOMAS FULLER

If you have to make
mistakes, make them good
and big, don't be middling in
anything if you can help it.

—HILDEGARD KNEF

TEACHERS SHOULD UNMASK THEM-
SELVES, ADMIT INTO CONSCIOUSNESS
THE IDEA THAT ONE DOES NOT NEED TO
KNOW EVERYTHING THERE IS TO KNOW AND
ONE DOES NOT HAVE TO PRETEND TO KNOW
EVERYTHING THERE IS TO KNOW.

—ESTHER P. ROTHMAN

Above all things we must take care that the child, who is not yet old enough to love his studies, does not come to hate them and dread the bitterness which he once tasted, even when the years of infancy are left behind. His studies must be made an amusement.

—Marcus Fabius Quintilianus

IF YOU PROMISE NOT TO BELIEVE EVERY-THING YOUR CHILD SAYS HAPPENS AT THIS SCHOOL, I'LL PROMISE NOT TO BELIEVE EVERYTHING HE SAYS HAPPENS AT HOME.

—ANONYMOUS

The pupil who is never required to do what he cannot do, never does what he can do.

—JOHN STUART MILL

Setting an example is

not the main means of

influencing another, it is

the only means.

—ALBERT EINSTEIN

The potential possibilities
of any child are the most
intriguing and stimulating
in all creation.

—RAY L. WILBUR

We must nurture our children

with confidence. They can't

make it if they are constantly

told that they won't.

—GEORGE CLEMENTS

The secret of education

is respecting the pupil.

—RALPH WALDO EMERSON

TO HELP THE CHILD IN ITS OWN BATTLE, TO STRENGTHEN IT AND EQUIP IT, NOT FOR SOME OUTSIDE END PROPOSED BY THE STATE, OR BY ANY OTHER IMPERSONAL AUTHORITY, BUT TO THE ENDS WHICH THE CHILD'S OWN SPIRIT IS OBSCURELY SEEKING.

—BERTRAND RUSSELL

If you would hit the mark,

you must aim a little above it;

every arrow that flies feels the

attraction of earth.

—HENRY WADSWORTH LONGFELLOW

A CHILD MUST FEEL THE FLUSH OF VIC-TORY AND THE HEART-SINKING OF DISAPPOINTMENT BEFORE HE TAKES WITH A WILL TO THE TASKS DISTASTEFUL TO HIM AND RESOLVES TO DANCE HIS WAY THROUGH A DULL ROUTINE OF TEXTBOOKS.

—HELEN KELLER

Education is helping the child realize his potentialities.

—ERICH FROMM

The greatest sign of success

for a teacher . . . is to be able

to say, "The children are now

working as if I did not exist."

—MARIA MONTESSORI

At the desk where I sit, I have learned one great truth. The answer for all our national problems—the answer for all the problems of the world—comes to a single word. That word is "education."

—Lyndon B. Johnson

The most extraordinary thing
about a really good teacher
is that he or she transcends
accepted educational methods.

—MARGARET MEAD

When I teach people

I marry them.

—Sylvia Ashton-Warner

Sixty years ago I knew every-thing; now I know nothing; education is a progressive discovery of our own ignorance.

—WILL DURANT

It is in our minds that we live much of our life.

—IVY COMPTON-BURNETT

My joy in learning is partly

that it enables me to teach.

—SENECA

I AM CONVINCED THAT IT IS OF PRIMOR-
DIAL IMPORTANCE TO LEARN MORE EVERY
YEAR THAN THE YEAR BEFORE. AFTER ALL,
WHAT IS EDUCATION BUT A PROCESS BY WHICH
A PERSON BEGINS TO LEARN HOW TO LEARN?

—PETER USTINOV

The test and use of man's
education is that he finds
pleasure in the exercise of
his mind.

—JACQUES BARZUN

Life is a festival

only to the wise.

—Ralph Waldo Emerson

LITERATURE IS MY UTOPIA. HERE I AM NOT DISENFRANCHISED. NO BARRIER OF THE SENSES SHUTS ME OUT FROM THE SWEET, GRACIOUS DISCOURSE OF MY BOOK FRIENDS.

—HELEN KELLER

A teacher must believe in the value and interest of his subject as a doctor believes in health.

—GILBERT HIGHET

Don't despair of a student if he has one clear idea.

—NATHANIAL EMMONS

IT IS IMPORTANT THAT STUDENTS BRING A CERTAIN RAGAMUFFIN, BAREFOOT IRREVERENCE TO THEIR STUDIES; THEY ARE NOT HERE TO WORSHIP WHAT IS KNOWN, BUT TO QUESTION IT.

—JACOB BRONOWSKI

There are no evil thoughts
except one: the refusal to think.

—AYN RAND

YOU CAN TEACH A STUDENT A LESSON FOR A DAY; BUT IF YOU CAN TEACH HIM TO LEARN BY CREATING CURIOSITY, HE WILL CONTINUE THE LEARNING PROCESS AS LONG AS HE LIVES.

—CLAY P. BEDFORD

TEACHERS BELIEVE THEY HAVE A GIFT FOR GIVING; IT DRIVES THEM WITH THE SAME IRREPRESSIBLE DRIVE THAT DRIVES OTHERS TO CREATE A WORK OF ART OR A MARKET OR A BUILDING.

—A. BARTLETT GIAMATTI

One good head is better than

a hundred strong hands.

—THOMAS FULLER

The true teacher defends his pupils against his own personal influence.

—A. BRONSON ALCOTT

*The secret of teaching is
to appear to have known all
your life what you learned
this afternoon.*

—Anonymous

WHEN YOU WISH TO INSTRUCT, BE BRIEF; THAT MEN'S MINDS TAKE IN QUICKLY WHAT YOU SAY, LEARN ITS LESSON, AND RETAIN IT FAITHFULLY. EVERY WORD THAT IS UNNECESSARY ONLY POURS OVER THE SIDE OF A BRIMMING MIND.

—CICERO

Teaching was the hardest work I had ever done, and it remains the hardest work I have done to date.

—ANN RICHARDS

A school should not be

a preparation for life.

A school should be life.

—ELBERT HUBBARD

I was still learning when I taught my last class.

—Claude M. Fuess

I'M NOT A TEACHER: ONLY A FELLOW TRAVELER OF WHOM YOU ASKED THE WAY. I POINTED AHEAD—AHEAD OF MYSELF AS WELL AS OF YOU.

—GEORGE BERNARD SHAW

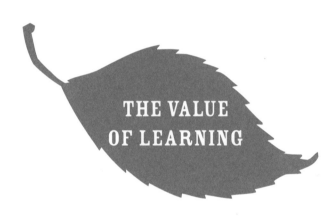

THE VALUE
OF LEARNING

It is not enough to have a good mind; the main thing is to use it well.

—RENÉ DESCARTES

E DUCATION IS LEADING HUMAN SOULS TO WHAT IS BEST, AND MAKING WHAT IS BEST OUT OF THEM; AND THESE TWO OBJECTS ARE ALWAYS ATTAINABLE TOGETHER.

—JOHN RUSKIN

The direction in which education starts a man will determine his future in life.

—Plato

Untilled soil, however fertile
it may be, will bear thistles
and thorns; and so it is
with man's mind.

—TERESA OF AVILA

The mind is more vulnerable

than the stomach, because

it can be poisoned without

feeling immediate pain.

—HELEN MACINNES

*An education is not
a thing one gets, but a
lifelong process.*

—Gloria Steinem

We just must not, we just cannot afford the great waste that comes from the neglect of a single child.

—LYNDON B. JOHNSON

Our progress as a nation can

be no swifter than our

progress in education.

—John F. Kennedy

The great end of learning is nothing else but to seek for the lost mind.

—MEG-TZU

On one occasion Aristotle was asked how much educated men were superior to those uneducated: "As much," said he, "as the living are to the dead."

—Diogenes Laertius

Ignorance is bold,
and knowledge reserved.

—THUCYDIDES

E DUCATION IS NOT A *PRODUCT:* MARK, DIPLOMA, JOB, MONEY—IN THAT ORDER; IT IS A *PROCESS,* A NEVER–ENDING ONE.

—BEL KAUFMAN

All growth is a leap

in the dark.

—HENRY MILLER

There is no royal

road to learning.

—EUCLID

A LIBERAL EDUCATION IS AT THE HEART OF A CIVIL SOCIETY, AND AT THE HEART OF A LIBERAL EDUCATION IS THE ACT OF TEACHING.

—A. BARTLETT GIAMATTI

No man knows

what he can do till

he tries.

—PUBLILIUS SYRUS

The more we study the more

we discover our ignorance.

—Percy Bysshe Shelley

*The things taught in schools
are not an education but the
means of an education.*

—Ralph Waldo Emerson

*To me education is a leading
out of what is already there
in the pupil's soul.*

—MURIEL SPARK

Many people would sooner die

than think. In fact they do.

—BERTRAND RUSSELL

The goal of education is the advancement of knowledge and the dissemination of truth.

—JOHN F. KENNEDY

EVERY AGE HAS A KIND OF UNIVERSAL GENIUS, WHICH INCLINES THOSE THAT LIVE IN IT TO SOME PARTICULAR STUDIES.

—JOHN DRYDEN

*The aim of education
is the knowledge not of
facts but of values.*

—WILLIAM RALPH INGE

THE MAIN PART OF INTELLECTUAL EDU-
CATION IS NOT THE ACQUISITION OF
FACTS BUT LEARNING HOW TO MAKE FACTS
LIVE.

—OLIVER WENDELL HOLMES JR.

Learning without thought is useless. Thought without learning is dangerous.

—CONFUCIUS

THAT IS WHAT LEARNING IS. YOU SUDDENLY UNDERSTAND SOMETHING YOU'VE UNDERSTOOD ALL YOUR LIFE, BUT IN A NEW WAY.

—DORIS LESSING

Education is simply the soul

of a society as it passes from

one generation to another.

—G. K. Chesterton

*See your sons
and daughters: they are
your future.*

—ONEIDA PROVERB

There is nothing like

a dream to create the future.

—Victor Hugo

HE WHO LEARNS MUST SUFFER. AND EVEN IN OUR SLEEP PAIN THAT CANNOT FORGET FALLS DROP BY DROP UPON THE HEART, AND IN OUR OWN DESPAIR, AGAINST OUR WILL, COMES WISDOM TO US BY THE AWFUL GRACE OF GOD.

—AESCHYLUS

In a free world, if it is to remain free, we must maintain, with our lives if need be, but surely by our lives, the opportunity for a man to learn anything.

—J. Robert Oppenheimer

Know thyself.

—PLUTARCH

It is all right to say exactly what you think if you have learned to think exactly.

—MARCELENE COX

That's what education means—to be able to do what you've never done before.

—GEORGE HERBERT PALMER

To throw obstacles in the way of a complete education is like putting out the eyes.

—Elizabeth Cady Stanton

In the long run of history, the censor and the inquisitor have always lost. The only sure weapon against bad ideas is better ideas. The source of better ideas is wisdom. The surest path to wisdom is a liberal education.

—A. Whitney Griswold

Knowledge is recognition of something absent; it is a salutation, not an embrace.

—George Santayana

Education is what survives when what has been learned has been forgotten.

—B. F. SKINNER

A child miseducated

is a child lost.

—JOHN F. KENNEDY

THE OLDEST HABIT IN THE WORLD FOR RESISTING CHANGE IS TO COMPLAIN THAT UNLESS THE REMEDY TO THE DISEASE SHOULD BE UNIVERSALLY APPLIED IT SHOULD NOT BE APPLIED AT ALL. BUT YOU MUST START SOMEWHERE.

—WINSTON CHURCHILL

EDUCATION IS A PRIVATE MATTER BE-
TWEEN THE PERSON AND THE WORLD
OF KNOWLEDGE AND EXPERIENCE, AND HAS
LITTLE TO DO WITH SCHOOL OR COLLEGE.

—LILLIAN SMITH

It is not impossibilities which fill us with the deepest despair, but possibilities which we have failed to realize.

—Robert Mallet

Education is not the filling of a pail, but the lighting of a fire.

—William Butler Yeats

You have learnt something.

That always feels at first as if

you had lost something.

—George Bernard Shaw

KNOWLEDGE IS PROUD THAT HE HAS LEARN'D SO MUCH;

WISDOM IS HUMBLE THAT HE KNOWS NO MORE.

—WILLIAM COWPER

T HE FIRST AND WISEST OF THEM ALL
PROFESSED

TO KNOW THIS ONLY, THAT HE NOTHING
KNEW.

—JOHN MILTON

A good education should leave much to be desired.

—ALAN GREGG

I would live to study,

and not study to live.

—FRANCIS BACON

Teaching kids to count is fine, but teaching them what counts is best.

—BOB TALBERT

A N EXTENSIVE KNOWLEDGE IS NEEDFUL TO THINKING PEOPLE—IT TAKES AWAY THE HEAT AND FEVER; AND HELPS, BY WIDENING SPECULATION, TO EASE THE BURDEN OF MYSTERY.

—JOHN KEATS

The highest result of education is tolerance.

—HELEN KELLER

The thinkers of the world

should by rights be guardians

of the world's mirth.

—AGNES REPPLIER

Learning is discovering that something is possible.

—FRITZ PERLS

Without knowledge,

life is no more than the

shadow of death.

—MOLIÈRE

Ah God! Had I but

studied in the days of my

foolish youth.

—FRANÇOIS VILLON

Readers are plentiful:

thinkers are rare.

—HARRIET MARTINEAU

More men fail through lack of

purpose than lack of talent.

—BILLY SUNDAY

*Education is a wonderful
thing. If you couldn't
sign your name you'd have
to pay cash.*

—RITA MAE BROWN

Great works are performed not by strength but by perseverance.

—SAMUEL JOHNSON

People get wisdom from thinking, not from learning.

—LAURA RIDING

L EARN TO READ SLOW: ALL OTHER GRACES

WILL FOLLOW IN THEIR PROPER PLACES.

—WILLIAM WALKER

*True originality consists
not in a new manner but in a
new vision.*

—EDITH WHARTON

Thoughts are energy. And you can make your world or break your world by thinking.

—SUSAN TAYLOR

Poverty of goods is easily cured; poverty of the mind is irreparable.

—MICHEL EYQUEM DE MONTAIGNE

The children of this world

are in their generation wiser

than the children of light.

—LUKE 16:8

LEAPS OVER WALLS . . . CAN BE EXTREMELY PERILOUS. TO LEAP SUCCESSFULLY, YOU NEED A SENSE OF HUMOR, THE SPIRIT OF ADVENTURE AND AN UNSHAKABLE CONVICTION THAT WHAT YOU ARE LEAPING OVER IS AN OBSTACLE UPON WHICH YOU WOULD OTHERWISE FALL DOWN.

—MONICA BALDWIN

They know enough who know how to learn.

—HENRY ADAMS

Genius without Education

is like Silver in the Mine.

—Benjamin Franklin

ALL KNOWLEDGE IS OF ITSELF OF SOME VALUE. THERE IS NOTHING SO MINUTE OR INCONSIDERABLE THAT I WOULD NOT RATHER KNOW IT THAN NOT.

—SAMUEL JOHNSON

The eating will give

you the appetite.

—Colombian proverb

Knowledge is power.

—FRANCIS BACON

*The object of education is
to prepare the young to
educate themselves throughout
their lives.*

—ROBERT MAYNARD HUTCHINS

Not to know certain things is a great part of wisdom.

—HUGO GROTIUS

T HE IMPORTANT THING IS NOT SO MUCH THAT EVERY CHILD SHOULD BE TAUGHT, AS THAT EVERY CHILD SHOULD BE GIVEN THE WISH TO LEARN.

—JOHN LUBBOCK

Education is the ability to listen to almost anything without losing your temper or your self-confidence.

—ROBERT FROST

Never be afraid to sit awhile

and think.

—LORRAINE HANSBERRY

NEXT IN IMPORTANCE TO FREEDOM AND JUSTICE IS POPULAR EDUCATION, WITHOUT WHICH NEITHER FREEDOM NOR JUSTICE CAN BE PERMANENTLY MAINTAINED.

—JAMES A. GARFIELD

*You should water
your children like you
water a tree.*

—HOPI PROVERB

Poverty has many roots, but the tap root is ignorance.

—LYNDON B. JOHNSON

Conversation is the legs

on which thought walks;

and writing, the wings by

which it flies.

—Countess of Blessington

Train up a child in the way he should go; and when he is old, he will not depart from it.

—Proverbs 22:6

'Tis education forms the common mind: Just as the twig is bent the tree's inclined.

—Alexander Pope

Once you wake up thought

in a man, you can never

put it to sleep again.

—ZORA NEALE HURSTON

THE GREATEST OBSTACLE TO DISCOVER-
ING THE SHAPE OF THE EARTH, THE
CONTINENTS AND THE OCEAN WAS NOT IG-
NORANCE BUT THE ILLUSION OF KNOWLEDGE.

—DANIEL J. BOORSTIN

EDUCATION THEN, BEYOND ALL OTHER DEVICES OF HUMAN ORIGIN, IS A GREAT EQUALIZER OF THE CONDITIONS OF MEN,—THE BALANCE WHEEL OF THE SOCIAL MACHINERY.

—HORACE MANN

Do you know the difference between education and experience? Education is when you read the fine print; experience is what you get when you don't.

—Pete Seeger

Education is hanging around until you've caught on.

—ROBERT FROST

The mind is like the stomach.

It is not how much you put

into it that counts, but how

much it digests.

—ALBERT JAY NOCK

STUDY IS LIKE THE HEAVEN'S GLORIOUS SUN,

THAT WILL NOT BE DEEP-SEARCH'D WITH SAUCY LOOKS . . .

—WILLIAM SHAKESPEARE

Education remains the key to both economic and political empowerment.

—BARBARA JORDAN

An unfulfilled vocation

drains the color from a man's

entire existence.

—HONORÉ DE BALZAC

Knowledge is the

antidote to fear.

—RALPH WALDO EMERSON

God will not look you over for medals, degrees or diplomas, but for scars.

—ELBERT HUBBARD

It is not enough for a man

to know how to ride, he must

also know how to fall.

—Puerto Rican proverb

Ignorance is not bliss—

it is oblivion.

—Philip Wylie

*In old days men studied
for the sake of self-improvement;
nowadays men study in order
to impress other people.*

—CONFUCIUS

The mind is an astonishing, long-living, erotic thing.

—Grace Paley

Instruction in youth is like engraving in stones.

—COLOMBIAN PROVERB

It is always the season for
the old to learn.

—AESCHYLUS

A closed mind is

a dying mind.

—Edna Ferber

Soap and education are

not as sudden as a massacre,

but they are more deadly in

the long run.

—MARK TWAIN

Only the educated

are free.

—EPICTETUS

*The ability to learn is
older—as it is also more
widespread—than is the
ability to teach.*

—MARGARET MEAD

The mind is slow in
unlearning what it has been
long in learning.

—SENECA

T HINKING . . . IS A SOUNDLESS DIALOGUE, IT IS THE WEAVING OF PATTERNS, IT IS A SEARCH FOR MEANING. THE ACTIVITY OF THOUGHT CONTRIBUTES TO AND SHAPES ALL THAT IS SPECIFICALLY HUMAN.

—VERA JOHN-STEINER

Any jackass can kick down

a barn, but it takes a good

carpenter to build one.

—Sam Rayburn

An educated man . . . is thoroughly inoculated against humbug, thinks for himself and tries to give his thoughts, in speech or on paper, some style.

—Alan Simpson

*Education is an
ornament in prosperity and
a refuge in adversity.*

—ARISTOTLE

No one has yet fully realized the wealth of sympathy, kindness, and generosity hidden in the soul of a child. The effort of every true education should be to unlock that treasure.

—Emma Goldman

A TEACHER'S
GIFT

Everyone who remembers his own educational experience remembers teachers, not methods and techniques. The teacher is the kingpin of the educational situation. He makes or breaks programs.

—Sidney Hook

Everywhere, we

learn only from those whom

we love.

—JOHANN WOLFGANG VON GOETHE

One looks back with appreciation to the brilliant teachers, but with gratitude to those who touched our human feelings. The curriculum is so much necessary raw material, but warmth is the vital element for the growing plant and for the soul of the child.

—Carl Jung

IF THERE WAS ONE EAGER EYE, ONE DOUBT-ING, CRITICAL MIND, ONE LIVELY CURIOS-ITY IN A WHOLE LECTURE-ROOM FULL OF COMMONPLACE BOYS AND GIRLS, HE WAS ITS SERVANT. THAT ARDOR COULD COMMAND HIM.

—WILLA CATHER

Housework is a breeze. Cooking is a pleasant diversion. Putting up a retaining wall is a lark. But teaching is like climbing a mountain.

—Fawn M. Brodie

WE EXPECT TEACHERS TO HANDLE TEENAGE PREGNANCY, SUBSTANCE ABUSE, AND THE FAILINGS OF THE FAMILY. THEN WE EXPECT THEM TO EDUCATE OUR CHILDREN.

—JOHN SCULLEY

TEACHERS WHO HAVE PLUGGED AWAY AT THEIR JOBS FOR TWENTY, THIRTY, AND FORTY YEARS ARE HEROES. I SUSPECT THEY KNOW IN THEIR HEARTS THEY'VE DONE A GOOD THING, TOO, AND ARE MORE SATISFIED WITH THEMSELVES THAN MOST PEOPLE ARE.

—ANDREW A. ROONEY

The things which hurt,

instruct.

—BENJAMIN FRANKLIN

Wit is the lightning of the mind, reason the sunshine, and reflection the moonlight.

—Countess of Blessington

If I had a child who wanted to be a teacher, I would bid him Godspeed as if he were going to a war. For indeed the war against prejudice, greed, and ignorance is eternal, and those who dedicate themselves to it give their lives no less because they may live to see some fraction of the battle won.

—James Hilton

Great teachers empathize with kids, respect them, and believe that each one has something special that can be built upon.

—ANN LIEBERMAN

EVERY MAN WHO RISES ABOVE THE COM-
MON LEVEL HAS RECEIVED TWO EDUCA-
TIONS: THE FIRST FROM HIS TEACHERS; THE
SECOND, MORE PERSONAL AND IMPORTANT,
FROM HIMSELF.

—EDWARD GIBBON

There may now exist

great men for things that do

not exist.

—SAMUEL BURCHARDT

I F THE HEAVENS WERE ALL PARCHMENT, AND THE TREES OF THE FOREST ALL PENS, AND EVERY HUMAN BEING WERE A SCRIBE, IT WOULD STILL BE IMPOSSIBLE TO RECORD ALL THAT I HAVE LEARNED FROM MY TEACHERS.

—ATTRIBUTED TO JOCHANAN
BEN ZAKKAI

The children need the

bread of the mind.

—RAFAEL CORDERO Y MOLINA

TEACHERS WHO EDUCATE CHILDREN DESERVE MORE HONOR THAN PARENTS WHO MERELY GAVE THEM BIRTH; FOR BARE LIFE IS FURNISHED BY THE ONE, THE OTHER ENSURES A GOOD LIFE.

—ARISTOTLE

THE FLASH OF INTELLECT EXPIRES,

UNLESS IT MEET CONGENIAL FIRES.

—HANNAH MORE

WE HAVE LEARNT THAT NOTHING IS SIMPLE AND RATIONAL EXCEPT WHAT WE OURSELVES HAVE INVENTED; THAT GOD THINKS IN TERMS NEITHER OF EUCLID NOR OF RIEMANN; THAT SCIENCE HAS "EXPLAINED" NOTHING; THAT THE MORE WE KNOW THE MORE FANTASTIC THE WORLD BECOMES AND THE PROFOUNDER THE SURROUNDING DARKNESS.

—ALDOUS HUXLEY

The world's great men have not commonly been great scholars, nor great scholars great men.

—OLIVER WENDELL HOLMES SR.

I hear and I forget.

I see and I remember.

I do and I understand.

—Chinese proverb

THE KEY TO EVERYTHING IS PATIENCE. YOU GET THE CHICKEN BY HATCHING THE EGG—NOT BY SMASHING IT.

—ELLEN GLASGOW

WHAT OFFICE IS THERE WHICH INVOLVES MORE RESPONSIBILITY, WHICH REQUIRES MORE QUALIFICATIONS, AND WHICH OUGHT, THEREFORE, TO BE MORE HONORABLE, THAN THAT OF TEACHING?

—HARRIET MARTINEAU

One good

schoolmaster is worth

a thousand priests.

—ROBERT G. INGERSOLL

TEACHER: TWO KINDS: THE KIND THAT FILL YOU WITH SO MUCH QUAIL SHOT THAT YOU CAN'T MOVE, AND THE KIND THAT JUST GIVE YOU A LITTLE PROD BEHIND AND YOU JUMP TO THE SKIES.

—ROBERT FROST

We lov'd the doctrine for the

teacher's sake.

—DANIEL DEFOE

THE GAINS IN EDUCATION ARE NEVER REALLY LOST. BOOKS MAY BE BURNED AND CITIES SACKED, BUT TRUTH, LIKE THE YEARNING FOR FREEDOM, LIVES IN THE HEARTS OF HUMBLE MEN.

—FRANKLIN D. ROOSEVELT

A teacher is better

than two books.

—GERMAN PROVERB

FOR RIGOROUS TEACHERS SEIZED MY YOUTH,

AND PURGED ITS FAITH, AND TRIMMED ITS FIRE,

SHOWED ME THE HIGH, WHITE STAR OF TRUTH,

THERE BADE ME GAZE, AND THERE ASPIRE.

—MATTHEW ARNOLD

The schools of the country are its future in miniature.

—TEHYI HSIEH

YOU CAN GET HELP FROM TEACHERS, BUT YOU ARE GOING TO HAVE TO LEARN A LOT BY YOURSELF, SITTING ALONE IN A ROOM.

—THEODORE GEISEL (DR. SEUSS)

Learning is not attained by chance, it must be sought for with ardor and attended to with diligence.

—ABIGAIL ADAMS

I HAVE NEVER HEARD ANYONE WHOM I CONSIDER A GOOD TEACHER CLAIM THAT HE OR SHE IS A GOOD TEACHER. . . . SELF-DOUBT SEEMS VERY MUCH A PART OF THE JOB OF TEACHING: ONE CAN NEVER BE SURE HOW WELL IT IS GOING.

—JOSEPH EPSTEIN

*Everybody sets out to
do something, and everybody
does something, but no one
does what he sets out to do.*

—GEORGE A. MOORE

IT IS PARADOXICAL THAT MANY EDUCATORS AND PARENTS STILL DIFFERENTIATE BETWEEN A TIME FOR LEARNING AND A TIME FOR PLAY WITHOUT SEEING THE VITAL CONNECTION BETWEEN THEM.

—LEO BUSCAGLIA

No bubble is so iridescent
or floats longer than that blown
by the successful teacher.

—Sir William Osler

Education has really one basic factor, a sine qua non—you must want it.

—George Edward Woodberry

The tragedy of life doesn't
lie in not reaching your goal.
The tragedy lies in having no
goal to reach.

—Benjamin E. Mays

THE FIRST IDEA THAT THE CHILD MUST ACQUIRE IN ORDER TO BE ACTIVELY DISCIPLINED IS THAT OF THE DIFFERENCE BETWEEN GOOD AND EVIL; AND THE TASK OF THE EDUCATOR LIES IN SEEING THAT THE CHILD DOES NOT CONFOUND GOOD WITH IMMOBILITY, AND EVIL WITH ACTIVITY.

—MARIA MONTESSORI

THE IDEAL CONDITION

Would be, I admit, that men should be
  right by instinct;
But since we are all likely to go astray,
The reasonable thing is to learn from
  those who can teach.

—Sophocles

Good teachers are costly, but

bad teachers cost more.

—Bob Talbert

FOR WHERE IS ANY AUTHOR IN THE WORLD

TEACHES SUCH BEAUTY AS A WOMAN'S EYE?

LEARNING IS BUT AN ADJUNCT TO OURSELF.

—WILLIAM SHAKESPEARE

*Give a man a fish and
you feed him for a day.
Teach a man to fish and you
feed him for a lifetime.*

—CHINESE PROVERB

*Any place that anyone
can learn something useful
from someone with experience is
an educational institution.*

—AL CAPP

JUST AS EATING AGAINST ONE'S WILL IS INJURIOUS TO HEALTH, SO STUDY WITH- OUT A LIKING FOR IT SPOILS THE MEMORY, AND IT RETAINS NOTHING IT TAKES IN.

—LEONARDO DA VINCI

It is with books as with men:

a very small number play

a great part, the rest are lost

in the multitude.

—VOLTAIRE

In the education of children there is nothing like alluring the interest and affection; otherwise you only make so many asses laden with books.

—MICHEL EYQUEM DE MONTAIGNE

THOSE THAT DO TEACH YOUNG BABES

DO IT WITH GENTLE MEANS AND EASY TASKS;

HE MIGHT HAVE CHID ME SO; FOR, IN GOOD
FAITH,

I AM A CHILD TO CHIDING.

—WILLIAM SHAKESPEARE

*Respect for the fragility
and importance of an
individual life is still the first
mark of the educated man.*

—NORMAN COUSINS

Some people are molded by their admirations, others by their hostilities.

—ELIZABETH BOWEN

AND IF EDUCATION IS ALWAYS TO BE CONCEIVED ALONG THE SAME ANTIQUATED LINES OF A MERE TRANSMISSION OF KNOWLEDGE, THERE IS LITTLE TO BE HOPED FROM IT IN THE BETTERING OF MAN'S FUTURE. FOR WHAT IS THE USE OF TRANSMITTING KNOWLEDGE IF THE INDIVIDUAL'S TOTAL DEVELOPMENT LAGS BEHIND?

—MARIA MONTESSORI

The regular course was Reeling and Writhing,

. . . and the different branches of Arithmetic—

Ambition, Distraction, Uglification, and Derision.

—Lewis Carroll

THE ONLY GOOD TEACHERS FOR YOU ARE THOSE FRIENDS WHO LOVE YOU, WHO THINK YOU ARE INTERESTING, OR VERY IMPORTANT, OR WONDERFULLY FUNNY.

—BRENDA UELAND

CHARMING WOMEN CAN TRUE CONVERTS MAKE,

WE LOVE THE PRECEPTS FOR THE TEACHER'S SAKE.

—GEORGE FARQUHAR

THE SWEET AND POWERFUL KNOWLEDGE WE GAIN . . . SHOULD NOT CLOSE US BACK UPON OUR NARROW SELVES, BUT SHOULD MAKE US TRULY "CITIZENS OF THE WORLD."

—NANNERL O. KEOHANE

Give a little love to a child, and you get a great deal back.

—JOHN RUSKIN

THE CLASSROOM AND TEACHER OCCUPY THE MOST IMPORTANT PART, THE MOST IMPORTANT POSITION OF THE HUMAN FABRIC. . . . IN THE SCHOOLHOUSE WE HAVE THE HEART OF THE WHOLE SOCIETY.

—HENRY GOLDEN

WE MIGHT CEASE THINKING OF SCHOOL AS A PLACE, AND LEARN TO BELIEVE THAT IT IS BASICALLY RELATIONSHIPS BETWEEN CHILDREN AND ADULTS, AND BETWEEN CHILDREN AND OTHER CHILDREN. THE FOUR WALLS AND THE PRINCIPAL'S OFFICE WOULD CEASE TO LOOM SO HUGELY AS THE ESSENTIAL INGREDIENTS.

—GEORGE DENNISON

A child cannot be taught
by anyone who despises him,
and a child cannot afford to
be fooled.

—JAMES BALDWIN

THE SCHOOLMASTER IS ABROAD, AND I TRUST MORE TO HIM, ARMED WITH HIS PRIMER, AGAINST THE SOLDIER IN FULL MILITARY ARRAY, FOR UPHOLDING AND EXTENDING THE LIBERTIES OF HIS COUNTRY.

—HENRY BROUGHAM

Level with your child by being honest. Nobody spots a phony quicker than a child.

—MARY MACCRACKEN

Education begins at home.
You can't blame school for not
putting into your child what
you don't put into him.

—GEOFFREY HOLDER

STUDY, LEARN, BUT GUARD THE ORIGINAL NAÏVETÉ. IT HAS TO BE WITHIN YOU, AS DESIRE FOR DRINK IS WITHIN THE DRUNKARD OR LOVE IS WITHIN THE LOVER.

—HENRI MATISSE

From your parents, you learn love and laughter and how to put one foot in front of the other. But when books are opened, you discover that you have wings.

—Helen Hayes

Do not seek to follow in

the footsteps of the men of old;

seek what they sought.

—BASHO

*It is one thing to show a
man that he is in error,
and another to put him in
possession of truth.*

—JOHN LOCKE

WHAT ANOTHER WOULD HAVE DONE AS WELL AS YOU, DO NOT DO IT. WHAT ANOTHER WOULD HAVE SAID AS WELL AS YOU, DO NOT SAY IT; WHAT ANOTHER WOULD HAVE WRITTEN AS WELL, DO NOT WRITE IT. BE FAITHFUL TO THAT WHICH EXISTS NOWHERE BUT IN YOURSELF—AND THUS MAKE YOURSELF INDISPENSABLE.

—ANDRÉ GIDE

Learning is always rebellion.
. . . Every bit of new truth
discovered is revolutionary to
what was believed before.

—MARGARET LEE RUNBECK

Learn as though you would never be able to master it; hold it as though you would be in fear of losing it.

—CONFUCIUS

An educated man

should know everything about

something, and something

about everything.

—C. V. WEDGWOOD

A LITTLE LEARNING IS A DANGEROUS THING.

DRINK DEEP, OR TASTE NOT THE PIERIAN SPRING:

THERE SHALLOW DRAUGHTS INTOXICATE THE BRAIN,

AND DRINKING LARGELY SOBERS US AGAIN.

—ALEXANDER POPE

What we learn with pleasure we never forget.

—LOUIS MERCIER

That which is made forgets—
the maker forgets not.

—AFRICAN PROVERB

THERE ARE FEW EARTHLY THINGS MORE BEAUTIFUL THAN A UNIVERSITY . . . A PLACE WHERE THOSE WHO HATE IGNORANCE MAY STRIVE TO KNOW, WHERE THOSE WHO PERCEIVE TRUTH MAY STRIVE TO MAKE OTHERS SEE.

—JOHN MASEFIELD

W E SUCCEED ONLY AS WE IDENTIFY IN LIFE, OR IN WAR, OR IN ANYTHING ELSE, A SINGLE OVERRIDING OBJECTIVE, AND MAKE ALL OTHER CONSIDERATIONS BEND TO THAT ONE OBJECTIVE.

—DWIGHT D. EISENHOWER

He who would leap high

must take a long run.

—DANISH PROVERB

Every exit is an entry

somewhere else.

—TOM STOPPARD

THE CHILD LEARNS MORE OF THE VIRTUES NEEDED IN MODERN LIFE—OF FAIRNESS, OF JUSTICE, OF COMRADESHIP, OF COLLECTIVE INTEREST AND ACTION—IN A COMMON SCHOOL THAN CAN BE TAUGHT IN THE MOST PERFECT FAMILY CIRCLE.

—CHARLOTTE PERKINS GILMAN

Anyone who stops learning is old, whether at twenty or eighty. Anyone who keeps learning stays young. The greatest thing in life is to keep your mind young.

—Henry Ford

Do YOU KNOW ANY OTHER BUSINESS OR PROFESSION WHERE HIGHLY-SKILLED SPECIALISTS ARE REQUIRED TO TALLY NUMBERS, ALPHABETIZE CARDS, PUT NOTICES INTO MAILBOXES, AND PATROL THE LUNCHROOM?

—BEL KAUFMAN

A teacher affects eternity; he can never tell where his influence stops.

—HENRY ADAMS

A TEACHER WHO CAN AROUSE A FEELING FOR ONE SINGLE GOOD ACTION . . . ACCOMPLISHES MORE THAN HE WHO FILLS OUR MEMORY WITH ROWS ON ROWS OF NATURAL OBJECTS, CLASSIFIED WITH NAME AND FORM.

—JOHANN WOLFGANG VON GOETHE

MOST OF US END UP WITH NO MORE THAN FIVE OR SIX PEOPLE WHO REMEMBER US. TEACHERS HAVE THOUSANDS OF PEOPLE WHO REMEMBER THEM FOR THE REST OF THEIR LIVES.

—ANDREW A. ROONEY

Teachers are expected to reach un-attainable goals with inadequate tools. The miracle is that at times they accomplish this impossible task.

—Haim G. Ginot

I owe a lot to my teachers

and mean to pay them

back someday.

—STEPHEN LEACOCK

This book was typeset in
Mrs. Eaves, Filosofia, Ribbon,
and Shelley Volante by
Ellen M. Carnahan.

Book design by
Christina Newhard